Guidelines for Leading Your Congregation

FINANCE

Funding ministries that nurture persons in their faith

By Wayne C. Barrett and Donald W. Joiner
General Board of Discipleship

FINANCE

Copyright © 2004 by Cokesbury

This book is printed on acid-free paper.

ISBN 0-687-03708-5

MANUFACTURED IN THE UNITED STATES OF AMERICA

CONTENTS

Our Identity, Call, and Mission **4**

What Is My Job? .... **.6**
The Finance System
Theological Foundations for Financial Leadership
Membership of the Committee on Finance

The Committee on Finance **9**
Functions and Responsibilities
Overview of a Year's Work
Funding Your Congregation's Ministry

Key Roles in Guiding Your Financial Ministry **22**
The Role of the Financial Secretary
The Role of the Treasurer
The Role of the Church Business Administrator
The Role of the Annual Audit

A Few Points to Remember. **27**

Resources **28**

General Agency Contacts .... Inside Back Cover

Our Identity, Call, and Mission

Y ou are so important to the life of the Christian church! You have con-
sented to be among a great and long line of people who have shared
the faith and led others in the work of Jesus Christ. We have the
church only because over the millennia people like you have caught the
vision of God's kingdom and have claimed a place in the faith community
to extend God's love to others. You have been called and have committed
your unique passions, gifts, and abilities in a position of leadership, and this
guide will help you understand some of the elements of that ministry and
how it fits within the mission of your church and of The United Methodist
Church.

"The mission of the Church is to make disciples of Jesus Christ. Local
churches provide the most significant arena through which disciple-making
occurs" (*The Book of Discipline of The United Methodist Church, 2004,*
¶120). The church is not only local but also global, and it is for everyone.
Our church has an organizational structure through which we work, but it is
a living organism as well. Each person is called to ministry by virtue of his
or her baptism, and that ministry takes place in all aspects of daily life, not
just within the walls of the church. Our *Book of Discipline* describes our mission to proclaim the gospel and to welcome people into the body of Christ, to
lead people to a commitment to God through Jesus Christ, to nurture them in
Christian living by various means of grace, and to send them into the world
as agents of Jesus Christ (¶121). Thus, through you—and many other
Christians—this very relational mission continues. (The *Discipline* explains
the ministry of all Christians and the essence of servant ministry and leadership in ¶¶125–137.)

Essential Leadership Functions

Five functions of leadership are essential to strengthen and support the ministry of the church: identifying and supporting leaders as spiritual leaders,
discovering current reality, naming shared vision, developing action plans,
and monitoring the journey. This Guideline will help you identify these elements and set a course for ministry.

Lead in the Spirit

Each leader is a spiritual leader and has the opportunity to model spiritual
maturity and discipline. John Wesley referred to the disciplines that cultivate
a relationship with God as the "means of grace" and suggested several
means: prayer, Bible study, fasting, public and private worship, Christian
conversation, and acts of mercy. Local church leaders are strongly encouraged to identify their own spiritual practices, cultivate new ones as they grow
in their own faith, and model and encourage these practices among their ministry team participants.

Discover Current Reality

"The way things are" is your current reality. How you organize, who does what, how bills get paid and plans get made are all building blocks of your current reality. Spend time with people who have been in this ministry and with your committee members to assess their view of how things are. Use "Christian conversation," one of the means of grace, not only to talk to others openly about their understanding of current reality but also to listen for the voice of God regarding your area of ministry.

Name Shared Vision

"The way things are" is only a prelude to "the way you want things to be." When the church is truly of God, it is the way God would envision it to be. Spend time with your committee and with other leaders in the church to discern the best and most faithful future you can imagine. How can you together identify your role and place in a faithful community that extends itself in its fourfold mission of reaching out and receiving people in the name of God, relating people to God, nurturing them in Christ and Christian living, and sending them forth as ministers into the world? Examine your committee's role and its place in that big picture and try to see yourselves as God's agents of grace and love.

Develop Action Plans

How do you get from here (your current reality) to there (your shared vision)? As a leader, one of your tasks is to hold in view both what is and what is hoped for so that you can build bridges to the future. These bridges are the interim goals and the action plans needed to accomplish the goals that will make your vision a reality. Remember that God may open up many (or different) avenues to that future, so be flexible and open to setting new goals and accepting new challenges. Action plans that describe how to meet interim goals should be specific, measurable, and attainable. While it is faithful to allow for the wondrous work of God in setting out bold plans, balance that boldness with realism. You and your committee will find information and tips here on developing and implementing the shared vision, the goals toward that vision, and the specific action plans that will accomplish the goals.

Monitor the Journey

A fifth responsibility of leaders is to keep an eye on how things are going. Setbacks will surely occur, but effective leaders keep moving toward their envisioned future. Not only will you monitor the progress of your committee's action plans to a faithful future but you will also be called to evaluate them in light of the ministry of the rest of the church. Immerse yourself and your plans in God's love and care. Voices from the congregation (both pro and con) may be the nudging of God to shift direction, rethink or plan, or move ahead boldly and without fear. Faithful leaders are attentive to the discernment of the congregation and to the heart of God in fulfilling the mission of the church.

What Is My Job?

T he job of the committee on finance is to identify, perfect, and manage the finance system for the congregation. The finance system is the processes of raising, managing, and dispersing the finances so that the mission and vision of the congregation can be achieved.

Key participants within the finance system include the chairperson of the committee on finance, for whom most of this Guideline is intended. In addition, the financial secretary, treasurer, and church business administrator will benefit from this volume, and there is a section devoted to their roles as well, beginning on page 22.

The Finance System

The Finance System

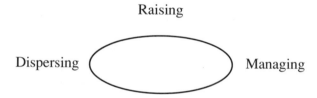

Your job as chair of the committee on finance is to ensure that these financial processes are completed. Meet with the former chair of the committee on finance, the pastor, the lay leader, and the chair of the church council to get their understanding of this financial system.

Although local needs will determine how often your committee meets, you should schedule meetings for the entire year. Inform each member of the meeting dates. The importance of meeting on a regular basis cannot be emphasized enough. Whatever the size of your congregation, your committee needs to meet regularly to be fully aware of the financial condition of your church, to manage the funds that are received, and to plan for adequate funding for the church's mission.

At Your Committee's First Meeting of the Year:

1. Review these Guidelines.
2. Study the mission and vision of your church and determine how your work will assist the church in the accomplishment of the mission and vision.
3. Have the committee identify goals for the year. These goals might include:
   - when and how you will develop the annual budget
   - when and how to conduct the annual fund campaign
   - when and how the treasurer and financial secretary should report
   - how much of the annual income should be reached by the end of each quarter
   - what will be done about any shortfall in expected income
   - when the annual audit will be completed and by whom.
4. Report to the church council or board. The committee should meet far enough in advance of each regular session of the church council or board to enable it to develop a complete report on the financial status of the church.
5. Develop a plan for the year's work, including a schedule of future meetings. Although your job is to call the meetings of this committee, to set the agenda, and to run the meetings, as well as to see the overall picture of the financial process as described in this Guideline, you will also want to care for the spiritual formation of those who are part of your committee.

Theological Foundations for Financial Leadership

The Bible speaks frequently about money and wealth and emphasizes the importance of generous giving (see Proverbs 22:16; 2 Corinthians 8–9), wise investment (see Luke 16:10-13); debt management (see Proverbs 21:20; 22:7), prudent fiscal oversight (see Luke 12:13-21; Acts 4:32-35); and appropriate attitude (see 1 Timothy 6:10). As the chairperson of the committee on finance, you have at the heart of your task providing for the ministry of your church through wise money management. Whatever income and expense is generated by the church is ultimately for the work of ministry.

The task of providing leadership for the financial ministry of the congregation has been recognized for nearly 300 years of Methodist history. John Wesley established key leaders within each congregation, the *stewards,* who were responsible for seeing that the ministry would have financial support. It was a great honor and an awesome responsibility to be designated a steward.

From the earliest days of our church's history, stewards recognized the profound *spiritual* nature of giving within the life of the congregation. While enormous demographic changes have occurred over the centuries, the fact that giving reflects a spiritual commitment to Jesus Christ is as true today as it was in the eighteenth century. The ministry of finance in a United Methodist congregation will be influenced, more than anything else, by our success in demonstrating the spiritual connection between the *offering* and the ministry it enables. To be called into the financial ministry of the church is to do holy work.

A critical component of this ministry is recognition of the historic differences between Christian stewardship and funding ministry. Funding ministry, often called "fundraising," consists of the varied tasks associated with gathering funds to enable ministry to take place. Underlying and supporting these tasks, however, is the conceptual discipline of stewardship. In our tradition, we understand ourselves as stewards who respond to our giftedness. It is this balance between the "what" (fundraising) and the "why" (stewardship) that is the genius of Wesleyan financial leadership.

Whether our task is soliciting, allocating, managing, or dispersing the funds for ministry, finance leaders act as extensions of the stewardship of God's people.

Membership of the Committee on Finance

As a member of the committee on finance you are part of a team. At its best, the team functions in such a way that the whole becomes greater than the sum of the parts. This is not only because of the way the finance committee draws its strength from its broad representation but also because of its fundamental commitment to corporate stewardship.

The *Book of Discipline* provides for the committee on finance to be made up of persons who, by virtue of other leadership responsibilities, link the committee to other areas of congregational life, as well as several persons who are nominated in recognition of their commitment and witness of personal stewardship. The *Discipline* calls for the following members of the committee:
● chairperson
● pastor(s)
● lay member of the annual conference (one)
● chairperson of the church council or board
● chairperson or representative of staff/pastor-parish relations committee
● representative of the trustees (selected by the trustees)
● chairperson of the ministry group on stewardship
● lay leader
● financial secretary
● treasurer
● church business administrator
● others as determined by the charge conference.
With the exception of the pastor, when paid employees serve on the committee on finance, such as financial secretary, treasurer, or business administrator, they serve without vote.

The Committee on Finance

Functions and Responsibilities

1. Providing Financial Direction

Responsibility for the financial health of a congregation is an awesome task. The congregation looks to you to provide for the underwriting of the ministry of its church. In providing "direction," you are demonstrating by word and action that someone is in control, that there is a plan, and that faithful stewards are leading the congregation's finances.

It is vital that you and your committee have a sense of direction, a plan to move the congregation's financial stewardship, and the ability to monitor the ongoing finances of the church. You may need to delegate some of the committee's responsibilities both to particular committee members and to key leaders beyond the committee on finance.

2. Providing for the Annual Funding Program

Although the funding ministry of your congregation is a year-round responsibility, most congregations need a particular time of the year when financial commitments are particularly encouraged. Even as you begin a new calendar year, it is not too early to be intentional about the design and leadership of this year's program. (Indeed, as more and more congregations move to spring commitment programs, January may be too late to begin this planning.)

As with any other component of the church's ministry, it is good to begin the strategizing by identifying the immediate need. In terms of funding campaigns, there are two generic goals to be considered:

a) increasing the number of commitments received (expanding the financial base)
b) increasing the amount committed by those people comprising the financial base (an "upgrade" campaign).

In the cycle of every congregation's life, there will be a time when each of these particular goals must be addressed.

Consider the "Giving Pyramid." This exhibit shows that three-quarters of the congregation's income can be expected to come from up to 33 percent of the membership. If your congregation's giving varies much from these norms without an obvious explanation (yours is a new church, for example), you may wish to remedy the discrepancy with this year's funding program.

THE GIVING PYRAMID

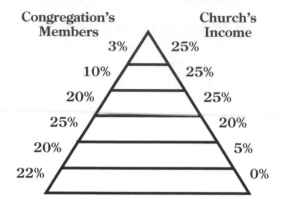

Congregation's
Members

Church's
Income

3% 25%

10% 25%

20% 25%

25% 20%

20% 5%

22% 0%

Campaign Timeline

Pre-campaign	Recruit leadership
Week One	Meet to establish timeline and theme and to assign responsibilities
Week Two	Announce campaign to congregation
Week Three	Meet to touch base and review progress
Week Four	Prepare letters and campaign materials
Week Five	Begin mailings; congregational members begin presentations during worship
Week Six	Continue worship presentations; committee meets
Week Seven	Call or visit each family; presenters continue
Week Eight	Organize Commitment Sunday service
Week Nine	Follow up: thank-yous to all who responded, calls to those not responding

See "The Annual Funding Program" (pp. 17–18) for more specific direction for this year's campaign.

3. Providing the Program Budget

Perhaps the most significant management tool that the committee on finance will use is the Program Budget. Creating and administering a fully funded program budget is one of the fundamental tasks of the committee. Let's examine budgeting from a church perspective.

What Is a Budget Anyway?

A church program budget is a management tool that assists us in providing financial direction for the congregation. The budget becomes an expression of who you are as a congregation and what you are about in our mutual ministry.

ABCs of Church Budgeting

Start with the congregation's vision of ministry. Do you have a mission statement? If so, that is the basis from which the budgeting process must proceed. If the congregation has no such statement, look for direction from the church council. Until you have such a statement, your budget will be little more than financial "guesses."

Invite broad-based input into the process of creating the congregation's vision and its goals. Goals take the concepts expressed in the vision statement and express them in a more definite form.

Healthy congregations invite input into this process from the widest possible sources. This can create heightened "ownership" of the program and increased commitment to its support. The diagram below highlights the way groups and individuals are provided with access to the budgetary process.

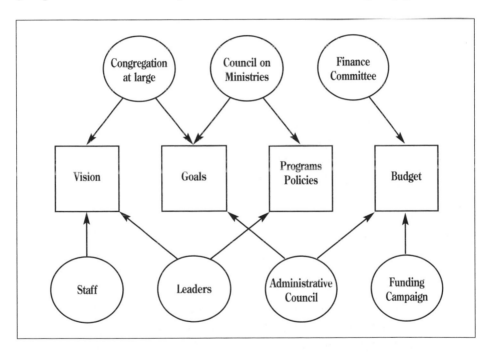

Early in the process it is desirable to invite the program work areas to submit their funding requests. Ask for a narrative description of each spending category so that there should be no misunderstanding regarding the purposes for the funding being requested.

The budget must be an internal document until the pledges are received. In spite of the popular practice of sending out copies of a proposed budget as a promotional piece during the commitment campaign, the budget is merely an internal document thus far. *Prematurely distributing a budget that is not yet funded invites misunderstanding, confusion, and potential disaster.*

After the financial commitments have been received, it is time to create the line-item budget. Begin with the expected income. In addition to the pledges, there is likely to be income from non-pledging donors, interest income, rentals, and fees. You can begin to build the program budget based upon the anticipated income.

4. Providing Financial Communications

Keeping the channels of communication open can do a great deal to improve the financial environment of the congregation. As in all communication, the best type is *two-way* communication. In all you do, strive for a combination of sharing *and* inviting information. Consider the following media for communicating your message:

> *A. The Worship Bulletin.* Probably no other medium offers the same level of regular, timely feedback as the weekly worship bulletin. This tool alone offers fifty-two chances to share important information. Be creative! Show more than the numbers.

> *B. Offertory Sentences and Announcements.* The time of the offering can be a splendid time for reinforcement of the act of giving. Report on current budgetary progress as the offering is about to be received.

> *C. Church Newsletter.* Make your communication *news.* Numbers and tables seldom communicate to the rank and file. Describe your efforts to deal with whatever your financial reality may be. Say "thank you" a lot. It really helps!

> *D. Giving Statements.* This may be the most useful and flexible vehicle for reinforcing, encouraging, and inviting increased giving.

> *E. Treasurer's Report.* Probably no document represents more effort to create by the treasurer and less to appreciate or understand by the rank and file. Strive to include at least one narrative paragraph highlighting efforts to deal with financial issues—good or bad. Even when the current financial environment is poor, beware of placing too much emphasis upon negative factors. A steady stream of negativity from the treasurer's report results in a treasurer's report that nobody will read.

> *F. The Finance Chairperson's Report.* A common mistake is to allow the treasurer's report to be the only report. The Finance Chair's perspective can provide the context for hope and confidence. Remember that the congregation looks to you for assurance that, whatever the financial situation, someone is looking out for the congregation.

G. Results of Giving. Many congregations do a better job reporting how much is given than reporting the good things the giving enabled in the first place. Because most of us are not accountants, the figures are seldom as useful as a narrative relating the outcomes enabled by the offering. Look for ways to tell the stories behind the numbers. Tell about the lives that will be enriched by the project.

5. Providing for Financial Reports and Substantiation

The congregation looks to the committee on finance for reports, or signals, about the financial health of the church. It is vital that accurate records be maintained so that adequate reports can be prepared. A financial report should be prepared for each meeting of the church council or board. Whether this report is produced by the treasurer, the chair of the committee, or both, it should present both a current month and a year-to-date picture of financial activity.

Develop a system that will enable you to track the flow of all giving to the church from the time the gift is given until the funds are remitted for their intended purpose. See the section of these Guidelines describing the roles of the financial secretary and treasurer.

A critical role under current IRS regulations is providing donors with adequate substantiation of charitable gifts. *The Revenue Reconciliation Act of 1993 requires a more specific type of receipting than ever before.*

Substantiation Rules

Donors who make a contribution of $250 or more must have a "contemporaneous written acknowledgment from the donee organization." This written document should include the church's name (perhaps on letterhead) and provide the following data:
1. The name of the donor.
2. A total of all contributions for the year.
3. A listing of each individual contribution of $250 or more. (You are not required to aggregate smaller contributions that total $250 to trigger this requirement.)
4. A statement that no goods or services were provided to the donor in exchange for the contribution. (An exception, of course, is the "intangible religious benefits" provided by the church's ministry.)
5. A description of any non-cash property contributed.
This written acknowledgment must be provided to the donor prior to the date the donor's tax return is filed on or prior to the due date for filing, whichever is earlier.

6. Building Philanthropists

Throughout the history of our church and nation a relatively small number of people have distinguished themselves through their extraordinary philanthropic contributions. Where do these individuals come from? They are developed, nurtured, and grown in congregations all across the church. How? *Consider these specific steps to grow your own crop of philanthropic Christians.*

A. *Assume the best rather than the worst.* Perhaps the fundamental factor in nurturing people who see themselves as capable of outstanding generosity is the simple invitation to give. Few significant gifts occur spontaneously; most require an invitation or request. *The church that learns to invite its members to grow in their giving will begin to witness the very growth it asks for.*

B. *Assist members in planning their own finances.* In an era where more than a million families declare personal bankruptcy annually, where the typical family spends 107 percent of its income, and where few families have any formal financial plan, *you can go a long way in creating philanthropists by providing regular personal financial assistance.* Do not be afraid to start with young adults and families with limited discretionary income. These are the times when habits are formed. Persons who have been nurtured into the practice of stewardship early in their lives are much more likely to raise their giving further when their finances enable it.

C. *Recognize that all gifts do not have to be current gifts.* The time in life when most people are capable of their most significant giving is *after life.* Giving through one's estate continues to be the best way for ordinary people to become philanthropic. When funds are no longer needed for the ordinary expenses of life, we all achieve a substantially higher giving potential. Congregations that learn to be patient are often rewarded with extraordinary bequests. (Congregations that act as if the only welcome gift must be placed in the Sunday offering plate seldom receive significant bequests.)

D. *Provide the infrastructure for donors to receive the assistance they may require in planning their contributions.* Planned giving often requires the assistance of a development professional or an estate planner. If your conference enjoys the services of a Foundation or Development office, learn to make their services available to your members. These Foundation directors are not your competition. They are part of your team.

E. *Offer recognition when significant gifts are received, particularly from estates.* People who have been reminded of acts of philanthropy are much more likely to practice the discipline themselves.

F. *Practice the AFI method.* ASK FOR IT! No one knows how many wonderful gifts are never completed simply because no one took the necessary catalytic step of asking. Do not allow your philanthropists to remain *potential* philanthropists. ASK!

Overview of a Year's Work

A typical schedule may include meeting a minimum of once a quarter. Such a schedule might be:

January—March

1. Organize and set goals for the year.
2. Finalize the budget for monthly income and expenditures.
3. Evaluate the past year's process of raising and managing the church's finances. Make preliminary plans for the next campaign.
4. Review the current year's commitments (estimates of giving). Project your cash flow for the year, month-by-month, from all sources of income.
5. Make plans for any month where expected income will be less than expected expenditures.
6. Set guidelines and policies for spending the budget and paying bills.
7. Mail year-end statements so that they arrive no later than January 30.

April—June

1. Evaluate the first quarter's receipt of income and budget expenditures. Determine what steps, if any, are needed to respond to the current cash-flow situation.
2. Send out the first quarter's statement of giving.
3. Begin setting up the task force for the current year's annual campaign.
4. Discuss other ways your church can increase giving.
5. Anticipate. Does your church usually have low income during the summer? What can you do to reduce the summer slump?
6. Invite the board to begin the program-planning process.

July—September

1. Evaluate the second quarter's receipt of income and budget expenditures. What steps need to be taken?
2. Send out the second quarter's statement of giving along with a letter to the congregation explaining the church's financial situation. Tell a story about the church's ministry along with the financial story.
3. Hear a report from the task force on the annual funding campaign. What progress has been made, and what are the final plans?
4. With the trustees or the Endowment/Permanent Fund Committee, evaluate your church's will-and-bequest program.
5. Order envelopes from Cokesbury.
6. Begin the budget-building process for next year's budget.

October—December

1. Evaluate the third quarter's income and expenditures. What needs to be done to assure that all obligations will be paid by year-end?
2. Send out the third quarter's statement of giving, with a letter to the congregation explaining the church's financial situation. Include information or stories about the church's ministry and mission.
3. Hear a report of the final plans for the annual campaign.
4. Plan the year-end giving process. Members are seeking places to make gifts at the end of the year. How will you encourage members to give to and through the church at year-end?
5. Finalize the budget for campaign purposes.
6. Recruit an audit committee to audit all financial records of the church and make recommendations.

Funding Your Congregation's Ministry

1. The Annual Funding Program

While funding your ministry is, of course, a year-round enterprise, a special effort to encourage financial commitment is absolutely critical. A congregation that fails to encourage its members regularly and systematically to commit their resources is a congregation on the way to extinction. *Members whose giving is backed by a fundamental commitment are documented to give at dramatically higher levels.* In short, you cannot afford to go even one more year without a well-planned program for funding.

Please do not wait until fall to begin the planning for your commitment campaign. You will have better results by recruiting the best leadership if you begin early. Furthermore, it is human nature to be more objective and enthusiastic if your planning can be done before the plans must immediately be implemented. Churches often begin the process with high resolve only to jettison virtually the entire enterprise because there is not time to do it right. Plan on selecting your funding campaign strategy at least ninety days before implementation. If outside leadership must be secured or materials need to be ordered, even more preparatory time may be required.

As you consider a campaign model, recognize that there are only two generic strategies for increasing giving:

A) *Base Expansion Campaigns* are oriented toward increasing the number of pledging units.

B) *Upgrade Campaigns* are oriented toward increasing the amount pledged by current donors.

Nearly every congregation needs to do *each* of these campaigns from time to time. You need to understand which goal you are targeting at any given time. Only when you have an understanding regarding the purpose of your campaigning can you select a campaign type that has the potential to produce the desired results. Following is a chart that shows the target projection or the outcome for eight common generic campaign models.

Base Expansion	Upgrade
"Saddlebag" Campaigns	Loyalty Sunday Campaigns
Every Member Visitation	Targeted Visitation
Cluster Groups	Mail Campaigns
Telephone	Dinners

Saddlebag Campaigns—A predetermined number of bags circulate from one church member's home until the bags have completed a "circuit" of homes. When the bag arrives at one's home, one fills out a pledge card and deposits it in the bag before dropping it off at the next member's home.

Every Member Visitation—A group of trained church volunteers commit to visit every member of the congregation in their home. The purpose of the visit (usually conducted in teams of two) is to share the mission and vision of the church's ministry, to listen to the member's concerns and interest, and to secure a financial commitment for the coming year.

Cluster Groups—Similar to the Every Member Visitation, except these meetings are conducted in various neighborhoods so that members can attend one cluster meeting in close proximity to their home.

Telephone—Similar to the Every Member Visitation, only conducted one-on-one by a telephone conversation.

Loyalty Sunday Campaigns—A multi-week program designed to increase the baseline of previous donors. This program often includes lay testimonies during worship, stewardship-themed Bible studies and preaching, high-visibility posters, and themed material.

Targeted Visitation—Trained laity visit pre-selected church members. These members are asked to consider prayerfully a financial commitment within a specific monetary range. The goal of these visitations is to encourage people to take a spiritual step up in their generosity.

Mail Campaigns—A series of letters mailed to church members. These letters are written in a manner to encourage people to increase their giving. The letters provide written instructions for completing a pledge card. These instructions may encourage the member to bring the card to a worship service or to simply return the pledge card by mail. Some mail campaigns send specific letters to members based on their previous giving patterns.

Dinners—Members are encouraged to come to a dinner where the ministry and mission of the church are overviewed for the coming year. Typically, church members speak about the impact that the church has made in their own personal lives. A missionary or another church member may provide insight into the outreach ministries of the church. People learn about the ministry of the church and the financial commitment that is required to fund this ministry. Members are then given an opportunity to respond and to make an estimate of their giving for the coming year.

The "Cycle Theory" diagram below illustrates how a variety of strategies may be implemented over a period of years to produce superior results.

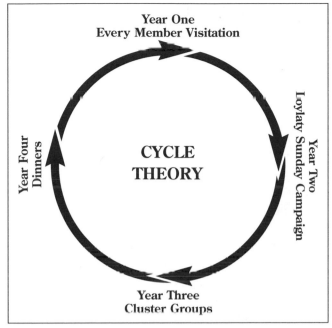

See the Resources section at the end of these Guidelines for resource materials on this.

2. Encouraging Giving Beyond the Budget

Giving that is generated by and through the operating budget should be understood as the foundational level of congregational giving, not as the limit of it. Indeed, giving beyond or "on top of " the budget can be the fastest growing component of your church's finances. Let's examine how you can prompt the giving to new levels beyond what is budgeted.

A coordinated budget should include ministries that the entire congregation ought to fund (undesignated funding), including administrative costs such as utilities, pastoral support, building operations, maintenance, and items that have no obvious core constituency for support. Other areas of funding (called designated funding) could be separated from the unified budget and isolated for support by a smaller constituency whose designated gifts will provide funding. (Make sure that designated giving does not erode the undesignated budgetary base.)

This kind of extra giving can finance benevolence, capital additions, acquisitions, and specific programmatic ministries. Before abandoning an item as unaffordable, churches should try to find individuals, or one person, whose interest in the project stimulates support.

The modern world loves, even demands, choices. A critical issue in many of our churches is the degree to which financial leaders are out of touch with this phenomenon. Often older leaders act as if this new attitude toward choice can be ignored or even repealed. They explain financial shortages as a "lack of loyalty" on the part of the younger generation. Such loyalty (if it ever existed) is, in general, in short supply today.

In today's world, our members are demanding **designated giving**. Our only choice lies in how we will manage these opportunities. Let's examine how congregations accommodate designated "second-mile" giving without losing operating income or enthusiasm.

A healthy environment for designated giving involves the enforcement of two principles. The first is this: It is OK to ask. Many financial leaders are reluctant to ask for second-mile giving. Sometimes they misunderstand what donors are thinking. Some plan their charitable giving months in advance. These careful givers often find themselves nominated to the finance committee. Because they dislike surprises and special offerings, they may conclude that everyone else feels the same. In fact, most people do not plan their giving months at a time, and they are willing to give more at another time. All we need to do is ask them.

It is not only OK to ask for support for designated second-mile projects, but it is *necessary* to do so. When Yogi Berra, the master of the malapropism, was about to retire, the Yankees held a special celebration for him. After being showered with gifts and applause, Yogi addressed the crowd: "I want to thank you all for making this day necessary." Necessary? In today's charitable-giving environment, asking for second-mile giving is necessary because our people require it and because it shows authentic leadership.

The second principle of designated giving is: It is OK to say no. Charitable giving, especially at the second-mile level, is a voluntary act. If parishioners do not feel comfortable declining a request, they will protect themselves by limiting the number of special offerings or even prohibiting them.

When a donor feels free to say "no, thank you," the second-mile fundraising process becomes less threatening. It also requires us to play fair in our fundraising efforts and not resort to high-pressure tactics, guilt trips, or manipulative behavior. In the long run, the escape option of saying no creates the best environment of giving—open, project-centered, and participative.

3. Encouraging Planned Giving

Perhaps the greatest source of potential increased giving is in the category called *planned giving*. Planned giving may be seen as the opposite of the weekly offering. While the Sunday offering is typically contributed out of donor *income,* planned giving is most often contributed out of donor *assets.* Because donor assets regularly constitute a pool that greatly exceeds the income of the donor (often 100 times the current income of the donor) the potential for giving is, similarly, much increased.

As congregations age, planned giving can offer a convenient and satisfying vehicle for aging donors to express their stewardship. Congregations wishing to maximize their financial resources while assisting donors in expanding their giving potential are encouraged to promote planned giving. Not only will you be providing a valuable option for your members but you will also be positioning the congregation to receive unprecedented levels of gifts.

Congregations are urged to contact their conference or area United Methodist Foundation for assistance in implementing their planned giving program. An excellent *Planned Giving Manual* is available, as well as consultation. If your conference is not served by a United Methodist Foundation, you may write the Planned Giving Resource Center of the General Board of Discipleship, P. O. Box 340003, Nashville, TN 37203-0003, telephone: 877-899-2780 ext. 7080 (toll free).

An excellent resource for churches to use in establishing a planned giving program or enhancing an existing program is *Achieving Dreams Beyond the Budget,* a planned-giving manual for congregations. This manual, presented in loose-leaf form, describes how to encourage "second pocket" giving, attract bequests and life-income gifts, and manage church funds creatively. You may also obtain this from Planned Giving Resource Center of the General Board of Discipleship.

Key Roles in Guiding Your Financial Ministry

The Role of the Financial Secretary

The office of the financial secretary is one of the most important and sensitive of the offices in the church. You were elected to this position by the charge conference by nomination of the committee on lay leadership (formerly nominations and personnel). Your role is more than a keeper of the records. The information you gather is important to the contributor for personal and tax reasons. That information is important to the administration of the church for planning purposes. It is important to the members of the pastoral staff as they minister to each member and friend of the church.

You cannot be the treasurer or related to the treasurer. The committee on finance will appoint at least two persons, not of the same household, to assist you, especially in counting and depositing funds. These persons cannot be related either to you or to the treasurer. *All persons who handle funds in your church must be bonded.*

Receiving Funds

As financial secretary, you will receive, record, and deposit all funds received by your church. Records of all deposits are to be submitted to the treasurer. A total of the funds that you record will correspond with the totals indicated in the records of the treasurer. Check your records with those of the treasurer at least once a quarter.

Work with the committee on finance or the audit committee to develop policies and procedures for handling all funds.

Record Keeping

You will keep two kinds of records: (1) records of moneys received and conveyed to the treasurer, and (2) records of all funds received from individuals and groups. A variety of prepared forms are available from Cokesbury to make your task both simple and accurate. Some churches design their own forms and have them printed to fit their specific needs.

Post individual records directly from the figure appearing on the envelope or check. Keep the records current! All records for each contributor must be kept on separate forms. There is nothing sacred, in itself, of the records you keep. That information should be available to the pastor, the committee on finance, and other church leaders (as determined by the church council or board) to administer the church and to minister to those people who are associated with the church.

Offering Envelopes

Offering envelopes have long since proved their value and are used by many congregations. They provide privacy to the contributor, a dated reminder to encourage regularity in giving, a basis for posting contributions to individual records, and a record for reference when a question arises about individual contributions.

As soon as the annual funding campaign has been completed, confirm the amount of each pledge in writing, the period over which it is to be paid (weekly, monthly, annually), and the beginning date of the pledge. Send envelopes (or send a monthly mailing of envelopes) to all giving units asking that they record their envelope number and put their name on the envelope for the first couple of weeks to assist in the accuracy of your records.

(A resource you will want to have is the *Local Church Financial Record Systems Handbook,* published each quadrennium by The United Methodist Publishing House.)

The Role of the Treasurer

As treasurer of the church, you have the unique responsibility of carrying out most of the financial decisions made by the committee on finance. Along with the normal duties expected of a treasurer in handling funds and keeping accurate records, the *Discipline* indicates that your responsibilities are to:

- *keep accurate and detailed records.* Columns and items in your records should correspond to those listed in the budget adopted by the church council or board.
- *disburse funds to the causes for which they have been contributed.* This is a simple matter of keeping trust with contributors. If funds are given for benevolent causes, they shall not be used to pay current expenses or other items in the budget. Funds received for nonbudgeted purposes shall be expended only for the causes given.
- *make monthly remittances to the conference treasurer.*
- *be certain that reserve (or escrow) funds are not to be used for current expenses.*

Relationships

As treasurer of the church you will be working with a number of persons and groups within and outside the church to make your job more effective—and enjoyable. As treasurer you will:

- be a member of the charge conference, the church council or board, and the committee on finance

- work with the financial secretary. You will receive from the financial secretary a voucher and deposit slip indicating the amounts deposited, along with the statement recording the sources of all funds received and the purposes for which they were given

- work with the chairperson of the committee on finance. Any questions about policies or procedures in handling funds should be cleared with the chairperson of the committee on finance. You will provide a regular report to the chairperson. Such reports become the basis of the regular report from the committee on finance to the church council or board

- work with the treasurer of the annual conference. Immediately after election as treasurer of your church, correspond with the conference treasurer to clarify your responsibility in transmitting funds to the annual conference

- work with your pastor, who is responsible for all phases of the work of the local church.

Make yourself aware of all the responsibilities you have to different governmental units. You can obtain a copy of the employer's tax guide from the Internal Revenue Service to assist you in federal tax matters. Federal taxes and Social Security (FICA) are to be withheld and paid on all employees except your pastor(s). The federal tax guide will explain procedures for withholding taxes and filing Form W-2 on all employees. If state taxes are to be withheld from employees' wages, be certain that you have the proper information and follow the recommended procedures.

Managing Funds

The way you manage the funds within your care will either build up or tear down the trust of those who give through the church. You symbolize the financial management system of the church. Careful record keeping, investment of unused funds, and timely payment of special funds collected for specific purposes will encourage persons to trust the church by giving more. Work with the committee on finance to establish procedures for paying bills (which bills to pay in what order), investing "idle" funds, and payment of special offerings.

Reporting

Regular reporting of all receipts and disbursements that flow through your books in an accurate and easily interpreted way is one of the most important responsibilities of the treasurer. This reporting includes budgeted and non-budgeted funds. You report to the committee on finance and, if requested, to the church council or board.

The Role of the Church Business Administrator

Expanding responsibilities for administration, as well as increasing state and federal regulations, are creating a need for additional staff to handle the business affairs of the church. The work of a church business administrator allows the staff of the church to spend more time on pastoral and spiritual duties. The church business administrator functions as part of the total church staff and is usually responsible directly to the senior pastor.

There is a growing pool of persons who have identified church business administration as a calling. These persons have a grasp of tools learned over a number of years in management. The United Methodist Church, through the United Methodist Association of Church Business Administrators, an affiliate of the General Council of Finance and Administration, works with these persons in a certification of their ministry.

The job description and employment policies related to this position should be developed by the committee on pastor-parish relations and approved by the church council. It is also the responsibility of these committees to recommend persons for employment to the church council.

Churches interested in learning about the role of the church business administrator should contact the United Methodist Association of Church Business Administrators, an affiliate of the General Council on Finance and Administration, 1200 Davis Street, Evanston, IL 60201, www.umacba.org; group e-mail: www.umacba@egroups.com.

The Role of the Annual Audit

Responsibility for the annual audit of all financial records is assigned by the *Book of Discipline* to the committee on finance. An audit is the best way for a local church to protect those persons elected to offices of financial responsibility from unwarranted charges of carelessness or improper handling of funds. It is not a symbol of distrust to have an annual audit; it is a symbol of support for their work.

What Is an Annual Audit?

An audit is an examination of all financial records to assure the church that all records are accurate. An annual audit assures that any errors will be corrected before they become too complicated. An audit assists those who are responsible for financial record keeping to discover new and better ways of doing their work.

An audit also evaluates the system for handling funds and keeping records and suggests ways to improve that system. Once a system of policies and procedures for handling and recording funds has been developed, the audit committee monitors the system to make sure it is what works best for your church.

When Should an Audit Be Made?

Normally the audit is made annually within one month after the close of the fiscal year or as soon as the financial records can be assembled. When there is a change of persons keeping these records, there should be an audit.

Who Conducts the Audit?

An audit committee shall be appointed by the committee on finance. This committee is made up of individuals who are not related to any person who keeps any of the financial records for the church. Some churches hire professional accountants for this purpose. If your church has members who are certified public accountants, bankers, or skilled bookkeepers, they should be approached to be on this committee.

Who Is the Audit Reported To?

The *Discipline* requires that a report of the audit be made to the charge conference. Your annual conference may provide additional guidelines and requirements with regard to the annual audit.

How Are Financial Records Preserved?

Preserve the records of the financial secretary, treasurer, and the annual audit in a safe place for at least five years. These records should be kept in a place outside the church building (such as a bank safe deposit box) for safekeeping. All invoices, vouchers, and canceled checks are to be stored for a similar period; they may be kept at the church in a safe, dry place. Each year the oldest set of records should be destroyed under the direction of the committee on finance.

A Few Points to Remember

*T*his is not intended as a summary but rather to lift up some points you will not want to forget. The page on which the statement appears in this booklet is included.

- Although your job is to call meetings of this committee, to set the agenda, and to run the meetings, as well as to see the overall picture of the financial process as described in this Guideline, you will also want to care for the spiritual formation of those who are part of your committee (p. 7).

- Responsibility for the financial health of a congregation is an awesome task. The congregation looks to you to provide for the underwriting of the ministry of their church. In providing "direction," you are demonstrating, by word and action, that someone is in control, that there is a plan, and that faithful stewards are managing the congregation's finances (p. 9).

- *Start with the congregation's vision of ministry.* Do you have a mission statement? If so, that is the basis from which the budgeting process must proceed. If the congregation has no such statement, look for direction from the church council. Until you have such a statement, your budget will be little more than financial "guesses" (p. 11).

- Early in the process, it is desirable to invite the program work areas to submit their funding requests. Ask for a narrative description of each spending category so that there will be no misunderstanding regarding the purposes for the funding being requested (p. 11).

- In spite of the popular practice of sending out copies of a proposed budget as a promotional piece during the commitment campaign, the budget is merely an internal document thus far. *Prematurely distributing a budget that is not yet funded invites misunderstanding, confusion, and potential disaster* (p. 12).

- *Tell the results of giving.* Many congregations do a better job of reporting how much is given than reporting the good things the giving enabled in the first place. Because most of us are not accountants, the figures are seldom as useful as a narrative relating the outcomes enabled by the offering. Look for ways to tell the stories behind the numbers. Tell about the lives that will be enriched by the project (p. 13).

- Remember the role of the annual audit. Responsibility for the annual audit of all financial records is assigned by the *Discipline* to the committee on finance. An audit is the best way for a local church to protect those persons it elects to offices of financial responsibility from unwarranted charges of carelessness or improper handling of funds. It is not a symbol of distrust to have an annual audit; it is a symbol of support for their work (pp. 25-26).

Resources

Funding Campaigns

• *New Consecration Sunday*, **Stewardship Program Kit,** by Herb Miller (Nashville: Abingdon Press, (2002). ISBN 0-687-06416-3). This new version of a popular fundraising program has helped many churches to turn their focus more on the ministry of the church than on raising money, at the same time increasing funds available for the ongoing ministry of the church.

• *Sharing God's Gifts* (United Methodist Communications). The materials in the kit draw from United Methodism's history and tradition to support God's claim on our money made real through local and worldwide giving that supports the church's four areas of ministry: nurture, education, outreach, and administration.

• *Step By Step,* by Kermit L. Braswell (Nashville: Abingdon Press, (1995), ISBN 0-687-01119-1). This is a complete program for increasing funds in the small membership church. This comprehensive guide takes church leaders from building a budget to securing the commitments.

Books and Other Resources

• *The Abingdon Guide to Funding Ministry* (2 volumes), by Donald W. Joiner (Nashville: Abingdon Press, 1996. ISBN 0-687-01989-3; 1995 ISBN 0-687-00477-2). A collection of the finest writings by individual writers across denomination lines. This guide is a complete reference book on funding ministry.

• *Achieving Dreams Beyond the Budget* (available from the Planned Giving Resource Center, General Board of Discipleship, P.O. Box. 340003, Nashville, TN 37203-0003). This exciting notebook provides all a church needs in order to organize, market, and tell the story about the stewardship of our assets and estates.

• *Afire With God: Spirited Stewardship for a New Century,* by Betsy Swarzentraub (Nashville: Discipleship Resources, 2000. ISBN 0-88177-273-9. Applies biblical foundations for personal and congregational stewardship.

• *The Book of Discipline of The United Methodist Church,* 2004 (Nashville: The United Methodist Publishing House, 2004. ISBN 0-687-03141-9).

• *Creating a Climate for Giving,* by Donald W. Joiner (Nashville: Discipleship Resources, 2001. ISBN 0-88177-318-2). Increasing funds available for ministry cannot happen until the leaders evaluate the financial system they have created. This book challenges the "old paradigm" of fundraising and assists a church to create a new culture where giving is part of the stewards response to a gracious God.

- *Don't Shoot the Horse ('Til You Know How to Drive the Tractor): Moving from Annual Fund Raising to a Life of Giving,* by Herb Mather (Nashville: Discipleship Resources, 1994; reprinted 1996, 1999. ISBN 0-88177-136-8). If your church is looking for a way to change what is not working, this book will help you move from annual fund raising to a life of giving for your church.

- *Extraordinary Money:Understanding the Church Capital Campaign,* by Michael Reeves (Nashville: Discipleship Resources, 2002. ISBN 0-88177-397-4). This exceptional book will help a congregation prepare for a capital fund campaign.

- *Faith & Money: Understanding Annual Giving in Church,* by Michael D. Reeves and Jennifer Tyler (Nashville: Discipleship Resources, 2003. ISBN 0-88177-410-3). Presents a theological grounding for working with the challenges, expectations, and attitudes of fund development.

- *Full Disclosure: What the Bible Says About Financial Giving,* by Herb Miller (Nashville: Discipleship Resources, 2003. ISBN 0-88177-411-1.) Explores twenty financial stewardship themes in the Old and New Testaments, along with contemporary applications of those themes.

- *Guidelines for Leading Your Church: 2005 –2008* (Nashville: Cokesbury, 2004. A set of twenty-six booklets (including this booklet and a booklet on stewardship) providing guidance for those persons responsible for the administration and program of the local church.

- *Holy Smoke! Whatever Happened to Tithing,* by J. Clif Christopher and Herb Mather (Nashville: Discipleship Resources, 1999. ISBN 0-88177-284-4). This book traces the history of tithing from its Old Testament roots through a more faithful understanding of the New Testament and provides Christians with a more contemporary understanding of tithing today.

- *Letters for All Seasons,* by Herbert Mather (Order Microsoft Word disk from h.mather@comcast.net). Provides sample letters for finance campaigns, monthly communications, and other times when the committee on finance communicates with contributors.

- *Local Church Financial Record Systems Handbook,* published each quadrennium by The United Methodist Publishing House.

- *Program Calendar* (United Methodist Communications).

- *Revolutionizing Christian Stewardship for the 21st Century: Lessons from
  Copernicus,* by Dan R. Dick (Nashville: Discipleship Resources, 1997;
  reprinted 1999. ISBN 0-88177-212-7). This book provides a vision for
  those churches that are ready to give up the past and push into a new
  vision of funding ministry.

- *Sharing God's Gifts* (free from United Methodist Communications).
  Provides easily accessible information about the structure and organiza-
  tion of The United Methodist Church and briefly describes its mission.

- *What Every Leader Needs to Know,* (series). (Nashville: Discipleship
  Resources, 2004).

New resources are being developed constantly. For an update and further
information, contact the Center for Christian Stewardship, General Board of
Discipleship, The United Methodist Church, P.O. Box 340003, Nashville,
TN 37203-0003; (877)-899-2780, ext. 7077; www.gbod.org/stewardship.